Date: 11/08/11

J 956.1 OWI
Owings, Lisa.
Turkey /

EXPLORING COUNTRIES

Turkey

by Lisa Owings

BELLWETHER MEDIA · MINNEAPOLIS, MN

BLASTOFF!

5

READERS

Note to Librarians, Teachers, and Parents:

Blastoff! Readers are carefully developed by literacy experts and combine standards-based content with developmentally appropriate text.

Level 1 provides the most support through repetition of high-frequency words, light text, predictable sentence patterns, and strong visual support.

Level 2 offers early readers a bit more challenge through varied simple sentences, increased text load, and less repetition of high-frequency words.

Level 3 advances early-fluent readers toward fluency through increased text and concept load, less reliance on visuals, longer sentences, and more literary language.

Level 4 builds reading stamina by providing more text per page, increased use of punctuation, greater variation in sentence patterns, and increasingly challenging vocabulary.

Level 5 encourages children to move from "learning to read" to "reading to learn" by providing even more text, varied writing styles, and less familiar topics.

Whichever book is right for your reader, Blastoff! Readers are the perfect books to build confidence and encourage a love of reading that will last a lifetime!

This edition first published in 2012 by Bellwether Media, Inc.

No part of this publication may be reproduced in whole or in part without written permission of the publisher. For information regarding permission, write to Bellwether Media, Inc., Attention: Permissions Department, 5357 Penn Avenue South, Minneapolis, MN 55419.

Library of Congress Cataloging-in-Publication Data
Owings, Lisa.
 Turkey / by Lisa Owings.
  p. cm. – (Blastoff! readers. Exploring countries)
 Includes bibliographical references and index.
 Summary: "Developed by literacy experts for students in grades three through seven, this book introduces young readers to the geography and culture of Turkey"–Provided by publisher.
 ISBN 978-1-60014-625-1 (hardcover : alk. paper)
 1. Turkey–Juvenile literature. 2. Turkey–Social life and customs–Juvenile literature. I. Title.
 DR417.4.O85 2012
 956.1–dc22   2011009538

Printed in the United States of America, North Mankato, MN.

080111   1187

Contents

Black Sea

Bulgaria

Greece

Ankara

Aegean Sea

N
W E
S

Mediterranean Sea

Turkey is a country that lies in both Europe and Asia. It spans 302,535 square miles (783,562 square kilometers). Most of Turkey is surrounded by water. The Mediterranean Sea washes onto the country's southern shore. To the north lies the Black Sea.

Turkey's western coast touches the turquoise waters of the Aegean Sea. Greece and Bulgaria are Turkey's neighbors to the west. Georgia, Armenia, Azerbaijan, and Iran lie to the east. Turkey shares its southern border with Syria and Iraq. Ankara is Turkey's capital city.

Most of Turkey lies in Asia. This part of the country is a **peninsula** called Anatolia. Mountains run along the edges of Anatolia. The Pontic Mountains are the main range in the north. The Taurus Mountains rise along the southern coast. Between the Pontic and Taurus ranges lies the Anatolian **Plateau**. Rock formations and **volcanoes** rise from this plateau. The Tigris and Euphrates rivers both begin in eastern Turkey and flow to the southeast. These rivers have been an important part of life in Turkey for thousands of years. The Turkish **straits** separate Anatolia from Thrace, the part of Turkey that lies in Europe.

fun fact

Mount Ararat is the highest point in Turkey. It is a 16,945-foot (5,165-meter) tall volcano.

Did you know?
The soft rock of Cappadocia allowed people to dig caves. These caves were used as homes, hiding places, and churches as early as the 300s.

Cappadocia and Pamukkale are great places to experience Turkey's history and natural beauty. Cappadocia is a region in the middle of Turkey with many unique rock formations. Over thousands of years, wind and rain have shaped the rocks into ripples, cones, and pillars.

Pamukkale is an area in western Turkey with huge cliffs. The cliffs are formed by **hot springs**. The hot water leaves behind a white **mineral** called calcite as it flows down the many **terraces** of the cliffs. This makes the cliffs look like they are covered in snow. *Pamukkale* means "cotton castle" in Turkish.

fun fact

The ancient Roman city of Hierapolis sits on Pamukkale. Tourists come from around the world to see the ruins and enjoy the hot springs.

loggerhead sea turtle

lynx

great bustard

fun fact
Great bustards are the heaviest flying birds on the planet. A great bustard can weigh up to 31 pounds (14 kilograms)!

Many kinds of animals make homes in Turkey's landscape. Bears and wolves chase their prey through forests and grassy plains. Other fierce predators include lynx and the rare Anatolian leopard. Foxes, boars, and beavers roam the forests. Gazelle and mountain goats dart up rocky slopes.

Mediterranean monk seal

The waters in and around Turkey are full of wildlife. Many birds stop to rest in the country's lakes and marshes as they **migrate** to warmer areas. Flamingos, pelicans, and herons are among the birds that do this each year. Loggerhead sea turtles near Turkey's shore struggle to find safe beaches to lay their eggs. Off the coast, the **endangered** Mediterranean monk seal swims in search of fish, squids, eels, and other prey.

fun fact

Turks have a lot of pride in their country. As the popular saying goes, "Happy is one who can say, I am Turkish!"

Turkey is home to more than 78.5 million people. Around 3 out of every 4 are Turkish. Their **ancestors** have lived in and around Turkey for over a thousand years. They speak Turkish, the country's official language. Kurds make up the second-largest group in Turkey. Around 1 out of every 5 people is Kurdish. They live in eastern Turkey and speak their own language. Arabs, Armenians, and Greeks also live in Turkey.

Speak Turkish!

English	Turkish	How to say it
hello	merhaba	MEHR-hah-bah
good-bye	hoşçakal	hoash-CHA-kahlen
thank you	teşekkür ederim	teh-sheh-KOOR eh-deh-reem
yes	evet	EH-vet
no	hayır	HAH-yuhr
please	lütfen	LOOT-fehn
friend	arkadaş	AHR-kah-dash

Grand Bazaar

fun fact

Markets called *bazaars* make Turkey a paradise for shoppers. Istanbul's Grand Bazaar is one of the largest in the world.

Turkish cities bustle with activity. Most Turks in cities live in apartments. Family members often rent apartments in the same building. People drive cars or pile into minibuses called *dolmuşes* to get around town. In the countryside, life moves at a slower pace. Families live in stone or brick houses in small farming communities.

14

The Islamic faith is an important part of life in Turkey. Most Turks are Muslims. Many pray five times a day. They are called to prayer with a special song. They remove their shoes and follow strict movements when they pray.

Where People Live in Turkey

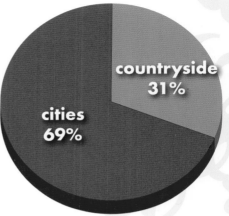

countryside 31%

cities 69%

Children in Turkey start school around age 6. Elementary school lasts for five years. Students learn math, science, history, and Turkish. Three years of middle school follow elementary school. Students prepare for an exam that determines which high schools they can attend.

Many high schools in Turkey focus on a single subject. Some teach students science or language. Others teach about Islam or prepare students for specific jobs. After high school, students can attend one of Turkey's many universities.

Working

Where People Work in Turkey

- manufacturing 25%
- farming 30%
- services 45%

Did you know?

Many Turks sell handmade goods. People appreciate the beauty of Turkish carpets, copper dishes, jewelry, glassware, and pottery.

In Turkish cities, most people have **service jobs**. They work in offices, schools, hospitals, shops, and restaurants. Hotel workers serve many **tourists** each year. Turkish factory workers make **textiles**, food products, steel, and cars.

Most Turks in the countryside are farmers. They tend fields of grain, cotton, or sugar beets. Olives and citrus fruits are plucked from trees. As hazelnuts fall to the ground, farmers gather them to ship to cities. Many farmers also raise cattle, sheep, goats, or water buffalo. Some Turks in the countryside work in mines. They bring copper, coal, iron ore, and other minerals up from underground.

backgammon

Turks enjoy spending time with family and friends. After a long day, many head to their local teahouse. They chat over hot drinks and play **backgammon** or cards. Some Turks like to shop at local *bazaars* and other markets. Many people also love to go to movies, plays, or concerts.

Most Turks are sports fans. Soccer is the favorite sport, but basketball and wrestling are also popular. Turkish wrestlers pour olive oil over their skin to make the sport more challenging. Skiers hit the slopes on snowy mountains. Many people head to the beach to swim, scuba dive, and kiteboard.

fun fact

Tourists visit Hierapolis to swim in the Antique Pool. Heated by hot springs, this pool is scattered with ancient Roman columns that collapsed during earthquakes.

Did you know?

Tea is the most popular beverage in Turkey. Tea sellers walk around selling tea to thirsty Turks!

Turkish families gather at home for most meals. A traditional breakfast is bread with cheese and olives. Lunch often includes soup, rice, or pasta. *Pide* is another common lunch dish. It is a Turkish bread topped with meats, cheeses, and vegetables. Dinner is the main meal in Turkey. It begins with appetizers, soups, and salads. These are often followed by meat served with rice or bulgar, a kind of wheat. Lamb, chicken, beef, and seafood are popular. *Baklava*, a pastry layered with nuts and honey, is a favorite dessert. Donuts called *lokma* are another sweet tradition.

fun fact

Food stands sell shish kebabs, sandwiches, and other snacks. Shish kebabs are meat and vegetables grilled on a stick.

pide

shish kebabs

Children's Day

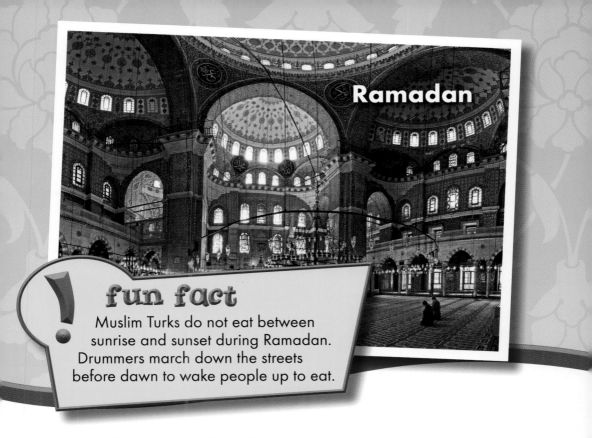

Ramadan

Turkey's holidays reflect the strong national pride of the Turkish people. April 23 is National Sovereignty Day and Children's Day. Children participate in events and parades that honor Mustafa Kemal Atatürk, the founder of Turkey. Republic Day falls on October 29. On this day, Turkish flags are flown throughout the country.

Most people in Turkey celebrate **Ramadan** and other Islamic holidays. *Şeker Bayrami*, or the Sugar Festival, comes at the end of Ramadan. People give each other candy and visit their oldest family members. *Kurban Bayrami*, or the Feast of the Sacrifice, is another important Islamic holiday. Many observe it by sacrificing an animal. They share its meat with family, friends, and those in need.

Mustafa Kemal Atatürk founded modern Turkey in 1923. He served as the country's first president until his death in 1938. Atatürk is still a large part of Turkish culture. Pictures and statues of him can be seen throughout the country. He is also featured in most school textbooks. Students **pledge** their loyalty to Atatürk and their country each week.

Atatürk introduced many **reforms** to Turkey. He believed in keeping the government separate from religion. He fought to increase the rights of women and improve education. The Turkish people's love of Atatürk is also a love of their country, history, and welcoming culture.

Did you know?
It is against the law to insult Atatürk. Any Turk who speaks against him or damages one of his pictures or statues can be arrested.

Mustafa Kemal Atatürk

Fast Facts About Turkey

Turkey's Flag

The Turkish flag is bright red. It has a white, five-pointed star and a crescent moon. The star and moon are symbols of both Turkey and Islam. This version of the flag has been used since 1844.

Official Name: Republic of Turkey

Area: 302,535 square miles (783,562 square kilometers); Turkey is the 37th largest country in the world.

Capital City:	Ankara
Important Cities:	Istanbul, Izmir, Bursa, Adana
Population:	78,785,548 (July 2011)
Official Language:	Turkish
National Holiday:	Republic Day (October 29)
Religions:	Muslim (99.8%), Other (0.2%)
Major Industries:	farming, manufacturing, mining, services
Natural Resources:	coal, iron ore, copper, gold, marble, clay
Manufactured Products:	cars, electronics, paper products, lumber, steel, textiles, food products
Farm Products:	citrus fruits, cotton, grain, hazelnuts, olives, sugar beets, beef, lamb
Unit of Money:	Turkish lira; the lira is divided into 100 kuru.

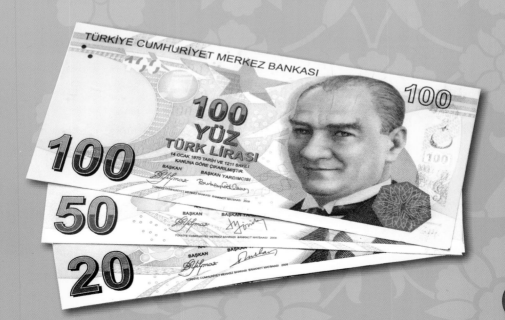

Glossary

ancestors—relatives who lived long ago

backgammon—a game of skill and chance played with a board, pieces known as checkers, and dice

endangered—close to becoming extinct

hot springs—areas where hot water flows up through cracks in the earth

migrate—to move from one place to another, often with the seasons

mineral—an element found in nature; iron ore, copper, and gold are examples of minerals.

peninsula—a section of land that extends out from a larger piece of land and is almost completely surrounded by water

plateau—an area of flat, raised land

pledge—to promise

Ramadan—the ninth month of the Islamic calendar; Ramadan is a time when Muslims fast from sunrise to sunset.

reforms—changes meant to improve something

service jobs—jobs that perform tasks for people or businesses

straits—narrow stretches of water that connect two larger bodies of water

terraces—areas of leveled land; terraces are cut into hillsides and look like steps.

textiles—fabrics or clothes that have been woven or knitted

tourists—people who are visiting a country

volcanoes—holes in the earth; when a volcano erupts, hot, melted rock called lava shoots out.

To Learn More

AT THE LIBRARY
Alexander, Vimala, Neriman Kemal, and Selina Kuo. *Welcome to Turkey*. Milwaukee, Wisc.: Gareth Stevens, 2002.

Sheehan, Sean. *Turkey*. Tarrytown, N.Y.: Marshall Cavendish, 2004.

Shields, Sarah. *Turkey*. Washington, D.C.: National Geographic, 2009.

ON THE WEB
Learning more about Turkey is as easy as 1, 2, 3.

1. Go to www.factsurfer.com.

2. Enter "Turkey" into the search box.

3. Click the "Surf" button and you will see a list of related Web sites.

With factsurfer.com, finding more information is just a click away.

Index

The images in this book are reproduced through the courtesy of: Faraways, front cover, pp. 18, 19 (right); Maisei Raman, front cover (flag), p. 28; Maggie Rosier, pp. 4-5; Franz Marc Frei / Alamy, pp. 6-7; Robert Harding Images / Masterfile, p. 7 (small); Emi Cristea, p. 8; Eileen Lennon / Photolibrary, p. 9; Peter Leahy, p. 10 (top); Kaido Karner, p. 10 (middle); S. Cooper Digital, p. 10 (bottom); Alfo / Nature Picture Library, pp. 10-11; Dave Bartruff / Photolibrary, p. 12; Luciano Mortula, p. 14; Dea / L Romano / Photolibrary, p. 15; Janine Wiedel / Alamy, pp. 16-17; Godong Godong / Photolibrary, p. 19 (left); Terry Harris / Alamy, p. 20; Japan Travel Bureau / Photolibrary, p. 21; Fabian von poser / Alamy, p. 22; Juan Martinez, pp. 23 (top & bottom), 25; Burhan Ozbilici / AP Images, p. 24; Terrance Klassen / Photolibrary, p. 26; Murad Sezer / AP Images, p. 27; Peter Horree / Alamy, p. 27 (small).